A Place For Betty & Other Poems

Lauren Poché

BookLeaf Publishing

India | USA | UK

A Place For Betty & Other Poems © 2022
Lauren Poché

All rights reserved.

Lauren Poché asserts the moral right to be identified as author of this work.

Presentation by *BookLeaf Publishing*

Web: www.bookleafpub.com

E-mail: info@bookleafpub.com

ISBN: 9789357444149

First edition 2022

DEDICATION

For my Mum "Betty"

Loved and missed always.

To my Dad,

Without your support, none of this would have happened.

I love you.

ACKNOWLEDGEMENT

Alzheimer's Society is the UK's leading
dementia charity. They campaign for change,
fund research to find a cure and support people
living with dementia today.

Dementia is the UK's biggest killer. Someone
develops it every three minutes and there's
currently no cure.

Visit

https://www.alzheimers.org.uk/

to learn more.

Lost

Who I am now, is not me.
Not what I am,
I'm forever a golden beach.
Years' worth of history,
washed away with the tide.

Remember who I was.
Take the smallest grain that I will forget,
carry me with you.

The moments - they come and go.
The next will pass with the oncoming wave,
it will hit you hard,
but don't let it pull you down.

Shiny specks, golden sands,
beaten by the currents.
CRUSHING

Carry upon a river my memories.
Through the creeks on your cheeks,
remember me.
Never forget.

Don't let it all wash away -

what we created.
For we existed.

Regards, Satan

Another face
faded
today.
Thank you, Al.
Let's go again tomorrow.
Zero fucks given.
Hell encourages
its parasite sent for memories.
Evaporate them all!
Regards,
Satan

Call me selfish

Call me selfish - for wanting the you that I knew

Call me insensitive - for thinking about how this
affects me and not you
Call me impatient - for not repeating myself
again
Call me ungrateful - if what we have isn't
enough

I'm just so used to this perfect picture memory,
it's hard to adjust
when I see you self-destruct.

There's no rhyme or reason to make this clear.
Because this whole thing is a dirty, black hole,
that's swallowing us all.

Every day I forget,
just like you,
the person that you was.

Today, all we're left with is questions, angry
words and hurt.
I'm afraid of the end.
Of faded pictures and treasured memories

becoming all that I have to hold.

call me yours – and when the time comes I will
remember for us.

Invincible? Not Quite

I wanna be invincible, so nothing else can break me.
Why can't I be invincible – Oh yeah, that only happens in fiction.
But even fiction has its weakness.
Superman's got the multi-coloured rocks.
The bat has his haunted past.
And Spidey's a geek, just like a lot of us.
Just like me, they fall victim to their hearts.
What's my weakness?
My weakness -- My weakness is you.

Memory Game

So, they say, that Mother knows best,
but let me tell you an unknown fact:
I struggle more than you know --
You think that I don't see the pity,
or the bitterness,
you think that I'm blind to it all – but,
I see you.
You may not think that I do,
but I do.
Oh, give me some credit please,
I'm more than this shell,
believe I'm still me.

Repeat yourself --
tell me things that I should know,
that you think I forgot.
I remember,
somewhere deep inside;
I hold all the pieces
of us within,
memories of times gone by,
dates of moments that we celebrate,
oh, all that we have to embrace.

Say: Say it again,
repeat it one more time,
don't let me down my friend.
I don't mean to be this way
but I can't change it,
if only it got easier --
Repeat yourself --
tell me things that I should know,
that you think I forgot.
I remember,
somewhere deep inside;
I hold all the pieces
of us within,
memories of times gone by,
dates of moments that we celebrate,
oh, all that we have to embrace.

But, I don't know how to let you know,
These things I say, aren't true,
at least, not always,
I never wished this upon us,
but life has a funny way of screwing us over.
Say: Say it again,
repeat it one more time,
don't let me down my friend.
I don't mean to be this way
but I can't change it,
if only it got easier —
If only we got a do-over,

to repeat it one more time.

Angel's Gallop

Never have I wept as much
since I was a child
thrust into the world
no longer hearing your heartbeat.
My head placed to your chest
replaced now with an angel's gallop.
I crave the warmth of your embrace.
So small I become
with only the echoes of your voice
in my memory.
Yet alone I must find a way
to hear your wisdom
from heaven's gate.

Anxiety

I'm battling in my own Royal Rumble:
Restless Mania
A triple threat fight, against
An - xi - ety.

Today's turmoil, the shops strike me
in an unexcepted chokehold.
It's a no-holds-barred
I   can't
tap   out.
I return to the car empty handed,
but at least I left the house today:
I'll take that as a win.

I refuse to be pinned; so pop a pill,
maybe I'll bring back
the groceries tomorrow.

More smack talk threw at me.
It's all fake, quit clutching your chest,
nothing hurts, it's all in your head.
Everybody hates me.
Body slammed: down for the count,
Count to five.

In Out, In Out, In Out
In   Out
In   Out

Back in this fight,
taking each day
as it comes.
Anxiety may knock me,
but it won't break me.
I got the groceries today.

Grief – A Haiku

In my sorrow, I
weep at a thistle blooming.
In time so will I!

Still Born

so much promise
four white walls once ignited hope
are now   suffocating
like the darkness taking over
the sun – now your heart endures an eclipse
once those first words were spoken
it felt like lions roaring by your neck,
every hair trembled to attention
your vessel drained of energy – it was surely a
mistake
just the hazy hue of labour's blur
hushed sympathies were ignored
but the silence told you it was real
so still   your son

no medicine could cure
the pain
a lone wolf abandoned
you wailed into the night

Home is not the same, your arms are heavy
but empty
like a hollow chest of gold - your heart
that colourful canvas bag

no longer something to treasure,
hides away
in the dark corners of the attic
like a nightmare
that nobody should encounter,
for the bud bloomed but never grew

Hello October

Like the torch with batteries fading,
those dark nights are flickering in.
An unsullied leaf floats on the breeze, it's
falling, fluttering like a new
fledgling flying for the first time.
One in a hundred would always
stand out. Like that one red, loose sock
that appears in the white wash.
Now a flaky addition to
someone's forgotten scrapbook:
October morning

Roaming Rose

The sun's rays burst through tattered curtains,
a once sleeping boy awakens, crying
for an absentee woman that never comes.

Evaluation – liability.
What heart she must possess; if one at all,
a roaming rose – its thorns unforgiving.

Permanent scars are always left behind
by a woman not fit to have the name mother,
and yet she continues to procreate.

Doomed starts for those innocents,
awaiting a hero.
To save them from this loveless dearth.

Love Struck

Like pins on an alley – strike!
Upon a careless throw,
what luck chances the clothes
as they scatter aimlessly upon the stairs.
The neighbour's shift,
anxious like a circus lion
trapped in a cage alone.
For the walls are as thin as gold leaf –
bloody delicate.

Agnes said leave them be,
even the horse that wins at Aintree
has to rest someday -
but I'm not a gambling man.
My racing days are long gone.
A greyhound locked behind a gate
ready to bolt,
but the lock's been sealed tight.
The loud noise grows: jackhammer, meows, hiss
such a feat for two ladies.

I strike across the living room floor – backwards
and forth,
but I'm no rocking chair, no rest for me.
The thought of payback crosses my mind,

forgetfulness and angina win out.
I sit and curse the youth – the 60s would be proud
of the neighbour's accomplishments.
All I want is a snooze on my lazy boy.
What do I have to do for such peace?

As luck would befall - although the terror I
never wished.
The unadulterated couple tumbled unaware,
consumed by the heat - they never turned it off.
It ignited like sparklers pirouetting
across every kitchen surface and beyond.
I awoke thinking it was the new blitz,
curtains and carpets an ashen mare
that never saw pastures green,
although Agnes always kept them pristine.

I call out to her and pray those ears are on for
once.
For I may never have raced again,
but every day I held the best prize of all.
Won by a fool: was her.

The dance of wolves

With every bend and
snap
I quake.
I'm thankful I won't ever have to do
the Lycan dance.
Their Ballerina's feet -
all   bloody and   torn.
Their tangoed clothes
Here,
There,
everywhere.
What success,
the final song
Belted out into the night.
Argh – woo
        ooo
        ooo!

DDA

DDA
Lizzy Grace

There's a sad small boy crying.
Sat at home.
Thinking of things he's too young to know.
Death aint a friend he's asked for.

Bright lights, loud noise.
Can you hear your friend?
No time for indecision.
That's him in your line of vision.

There's a numb motionless mum.
Sat at home.
She should be crying.
But death is a friend she expected.

Bright lights, loud noise.
Can you hear your friend?
No time for indecision.
That's him in your line of vision.

There's an angry distressed sister.
Gone from home.

Avoiding every memory.
Death is a friend she refuses to acknowledge.

Bright lights, loud noise.
Can you hear your friend?
No time for indecision.
Death waits around for no one.

I'm a Big Girl now

I'm a big girl now,
I know,
but they're times where I feel so small
and I just need my mother's hold,
but I'm the one taking care of you --
so I hold it all in
and be the one that you need.

Contour your face,
snap chat your day to day moment
it's the diary of the average girl's life
but that's not my story…

never been one to follow the norm,
yet sometimes,
I wish things could be so much easier
and I didn't have to teach you the things that you
taught me,
but it's funny how things come full circle.
I keep the smile upon my face,
so that no one knows I hurt inside.
You're the one that needs my focus now,
so let's make-believe and pretend we're 17 again
--
tell me stories of your younger days,

when you were burden-less
and just living in the moment was all that
mattered.

I never imagined this would be us right now,
roles reversed,
and I try so hard to be strong
but at times I look around and see just what we
could be --
it sucks,
there are no other words to say
that can make this sound more colourful.

I'm a big girl now
but there are times where I feel so small
And I just need my mother's hold
But I'm the one taking care of you
So I hold it all in and be the one that you need.

What a wonderful time of year

Holly, jolly,
Merry Christmas.
Until the time comes
for wrapping presents. Cursing
and paper cuts, running
out of sellotape,
a last ditch dash to the corner shop -
is often open late.
Santa Claus never had this much trouble.
Christmas comes but once a year.
Does everyone lose their marbles
until newyears eve?
Where we all make promises
we will likely break.
A kiss at midnight.
such wondrous delight
unless they had garlic.
Kiss me quick,
leave me faster,
oops, I ate pickles.

Solitude

I've worn solitude like amour
until tonight,
dreaming of space,

floating ---

Freedom, is that you calling?
I don't want to survive alone…
But these walls that I've built defy
even the Hulk's mighty smash.

Hello old friend,
is that you?
This choice is yours to make,
take a leap and –
fly!

Anxiety, in control

A horse gallops,
hooves to the groove.
Rapid laps around the cavities of my heart,
Faster --- oh!

And in my bed, bound I was for days on end,
Your face reappearing -
Still
Oh, so still.

The sirens wailed a banshee's cry,
a ricochet upon my heart.
Whose howls still haunt my mind
in the quiet - I, uncoil

Is this my just reward for a lifetime
of servitude – loving you
To be riddled with the lasting image of the ghost
of you?

So farewell has been long drawn out --
I'm still processing
this world of mine, without you
and my purpose now that you're gone